D1114803

Francis Stuart

THE IRISH WRITERS SERIES
James F. Carens, General Editor

GEORGE FITZMAURICE	Arthur E. McGuinness
FRANCIS STUART	J. H. Natterstad
PATRICK KAVANAGH	Darcy O'Brien
WILLIAM ALLINGHAM	Alan Warner
SIR SAMUEL FERGUSON	Malcolm Brown
LADY GREGORY	Hazard Adams
GEORGE RUSSELL (AE)	Richard M. Kain and James O'Brien
THOMAS DAVIS	Eileen Sullivan
PEADAR O'DONNELL	Grattan Freyer
OLIVER ST. JOHN GOGARTY	J. B. Lyons
SEUMAS HEANEY	Robert Buttel

FRANCIS STUART

J. H. Natterstad

Lewisburg

BUCKNELL UNIVERSITY PRESS

London: Associated University Presses

823
S 92 ₃ ᴎ

© 1974 by Associated University Presses, Inc.

Associated University Presses, Inc.
Cranbury, New Jersey 08512

Associated University Presses
108 New Bond Street
London W1Y 0QX, England

F ᴎ

Library of Congress Cataloging in Publication Data

Natterstad, J   H   1938–
    Francis Stuart.

    (The Irish writers series)
    Bibliography: p.
    1. Stuart, Francis, 1902–
PR6037.T875Z8   1974   823'.9'12 [B]   70–168817
ISBN 0–8387–7895–X
ISBN 0–8387–7979–4 (pbk.)

PRINTED IN THE UNITED STATES OF AMERICA

Contents

Chronology

1902 Born April 29, Townsville, Australia.

1909– Attended day school in Monkstown, County
1912 Dublin.

1912– Studied at various boarding schools in England.
1915

1916– Attended Rugby School.
1918

1920 Married Iseult Gonne.

1921 Daughter Dolores born in March; died of spinal meningitis in July.

1922 Participated in the Irish Civil War on the Republican side. Captured in August, and imprisoned until November 1923.

1924 *We Have Kept the Faith,* a short collection of poems, privately published in January. Moved from Dublin to Glencree, County Wicklow.

1926 Son Ian born.

1929 Moved to Laragh, Glendalough, County Wicklow.

1931 Daughter Katherine born. *Women and God,* his first novel, published.

9

1932   Published two of his most critically successful novels, *Pigeon Irish* and *The Coloured Dome.*

1933   *Men Crowd Me Round,* his first play, performed at the Abbey Theatre in March.

1939   Traveled to Germany in April to lecture and give readings from his novels at various universities; returned to Ireland in July.

1940– 1945   Took post as lecturer in modern English and Irish literature at Berlin University.

1945   Arrested by French occupation forces in November and imprisoned in Bregenz and later in Freiburg until July 1946.

1946– 1949   Lived in Freiburg, Germany, where he wrote and published *The Pillar of Cloud* (1948) and *Redemption* (1949), two of his finest postwar novels.

1949– 1951   Lived in Paris and published *The Flowering Cross* (1950).

1951   In the spring, moved to London.

1954   After the death of his wife in March, married Gertrud Meissner, whom he had met in Berlin and with whom he had been imprisoned in Germany.

1958   In April, returned to Ireland and lived there with his second wife near Dunshaughlin, County Meath.

1970   *Who Fears To Speak,* a play, presented at Liberty Hall, Dublin, in December.

1971   Moved to Dublin in August and published *Black List, Section H.*

Francis Stuart

1

Genesis of an Outcast

Like many other families from the north of Ireland, Francis Stuart's was of Scottish-Presbyterian origin on both sides and can be traced back to the settlements established in Ireland during the late seventeenth and early eighteenth centuries. His father, Henry Irwin Stuart, was born and reared near Dervock in County Antrim, where he lived until emigrating to Australia in his early twenties. On a visit to Ireland in 1901 he married Elizabeth Montgomery, a member of a neighboring family that had known the Stuarts for many years, and returned with his bride to the prosperous sheep station he had developed in Queensland.

The marriage between Henry and Elizabeth was short and ill-fated; Henry Francis Montgomery Stuart, born on April 29, 1902, in Townsville, Australia, was its only issue. About four months later, on August 15, the father died. The details of his death remain vague. In a letter to this writer, Francis Stuart described the situation: "The circumstances of his death in a mental home in Townsville soon after my birth have never been clear to me. Nobody spoke to me of him as I grew up. My mother was always silent on the subject.

13

I think he died from alcoholism, though it is possible
he killed himself during a fit of alcoholic depression."
The result of his death was that in December of 1902
Elizabeth began the long journey back to Ireland with
her eight-month-old son and his nurse.

These events occurring so early in Stuart's life would
have far-reaching consequences. His family had been
disrupted and would remain so throughout his for-
mative years. Almost certainly this accounts in some
measure for the later emphasis in his novels on the
value of small groups united by love and sympathy.
More importantly, his father was to become for him
a symbol of the outcast and the afflicted, with whom
Stuart himself was to identify. It is not surprising, then,
that Stuart came to see the serious writer as one of the
outcasts. His persona H in the autobiographical
novel, *Black List,* remarks: "A poet must be a counter-
current to the flow around him. That's what poetry is:
the other way of feeling and looking at the world."
Stuart would never give up his identification with
those on the fringe nor this view of the artist.

Once back in Ireland Elizabeth, along with her son
and his nurse, went to live with her sister, Janet Montgomery, at Shallon House, not far from Drogheda in
County Meath. This was to be Francis's home until
1909. The time he spent here in the seclusion of the
rolling countryside near the river Boyne was, as he
later described it, "an intensely absorbed and happy
one." There was his aunt, who was the only serious
reader and perhaps the only independent thinker on
either side of the family. It was from her library that
Francis obtained the books that held him "spell-

bound as a youth." Her independence also must have made some impression on the child: significantly, she was the only Stuart or Montgomery to become an Irish nationalist, the others remaining Unionists. Then, too, there was the comparative isolation of the area in which a quiet, introspective boy could find his own amusement and develop his imagination. Other adventures, like visiting the Montgomerys in Antrim, were not without excitement, but the return to the solitude of Shallon was always welcome. Most important of all, there was his English-born nurse, Nellie Farren, who provided the love and stability his own mother never offered, or was incapable of giving. Stuart was to write of her: "I had a nurse who came with us from Australia to whom I was very attached. My mother lived her own life and neither then nor later had I any very close bonds with her. She never resented my preference for my nurse and the latter became, in all but name, my mother."

In 1909, at age seven, Francis was enrolled in a day school in Monkstown, following his mother's move to Dublin. He remained there for three years before being sent to boarding school in England. Between 1912 and 1915 he attended three preparatory schools: the first, Bilton Grange, not far from Rugby, Warwickshire; another near Conway Bay in North Wales; and a third at Broadstairs, Kent.

The years at the various schools were emotionally disturbing ones. The freedom and solitude of Shallon, where he had enjoyed "the dreamy sort of days and idleness," had obviously not prepared him for the shock of the cold, rigid system he found at those "miserable preparatory schools." Moreover, for the first time he was separated from his nurse for extended periods, and this no doubt added to his sense of rootlessness. The depressing loneliness and the sense of being something of an outsider because he was Irish surely account, at least in part, for his lack of academic success and deep unhappiness.

There were other problems as well, which could only have aggravated the situation for a sensitive child. His mother remarried in 1913, and the stepfather, Henry Clements, managed to destroy the little stability remaining in Francis's life. In an interview Stuart recalls the event: "The result of his marriage was that I was separated from my nurse. I remember him saying to me once or twice, 'You're only a milksop,' or something like that. I know what he meant, and he didn't like the influence of my nurse, I think. I didn't get on with him. After his marriage he took my mother, and he kept moving all over the place." Now even the tenuous family relationship that had existed was further weakened, but the ties with Nellie Farren were never completely severed, although she moved to England and lived with her family. "During my holidays from English schools," Stuart wrote, "I often spent [time] with her and her family in England . . . . I was conscious of belonging to . . . the wrong family."

When he entered Rugby in January 1916, his attitude changed somewhat. Here, too, "every hour of the day [was] more or less mapped out," but he was a bit more mature now and was able to tolerate it, at least for a time. As he later remarked, "I think it had a good, toughening effect if you survived it. . . . I wouldn't say

I disliked it too much." Perhaps what made life at Rugby endurable, if far from pleasant, was that he found a kind of rough comradeship for the first time. There were others, he discovered, who felt themselves outsiders, and they formed their own clique, which insulated them to some extent against the life around them: "Well, we Irish and a Jew and a Pole," he recalled, "we made a little group, and it was good."

Although there was less loneliness at Rugby than at the previous schools, Francis continued to have academic problems. Remembering these days, Stuart has said: "I was told in some ways I was good, but in other ways [poor]. I got very bad reports from my four masters— not the only one to get bad reports, naturally, but the few who did were always in fear of being called up to the headmaster's room. In some instances it meant a birching, which is frightful." In the end he was, as he had feared he would be, sent up to the dreaded room, located in a tower of the main building, where he found the headmaster awaiting him with masters' reports complaining of "inattention and apathy," among other things. But to his relief he escaped a birching. In July 1918 he left school without being graduated. He recalls: "I was taken away. There was no point in leaving me. I wasn't making much headway. And then I got to the point where I used to go to the sanitorium—not that I was really ill, but . . . if you get to a point you can really become ill through dissatisfaction." So while Rugby may have had a "good toughening effect," Francis in the end did not really "survive it." He left physically and emotionally drained.

The disturbing years in the English public schools

must have been partly responsible for his later distrust
of all rigid, sterile social institutions, which he came
to see as perpetuating a deadly way of life and set of
values. His reaction to the news of the Russian Revolution indicates the direction his attitudes were beginning to take. A friend of his brought word of it
to him while he was in the sanitorium at Rugby, and
both were very excited by the event. As Stuart remembers it, the excitement came from hearing about something "explosive against the whole setup that we were
beginning to see was so unbearable. We would have
imagined into it, even several years later, a far more
ideal situation than it turned out." Clearly there was
more involved in this reaction than a schoolboy's
distaste for the English system of education: it suggested a broader dissatisfaction with the society he
saw around him.

There can be no doubt that during the last year or so
at Rugby he had begun to have serious misgivings
about the safe, conventional life of his Stuart and
Montgomery relatives in the north of Ireland. During
a visit with the Montgomerys, he wrote a letter to the
editor of Dublin's *Irish Independent*, arguing in favor
of Irish Home Rule. This was "not because," as he
observed in *Black List*, " . . . he had any great interest
in Irish, or any other kind of nationalism. What was
behind it was an instinct, far from conscious, to cut
himself off from the world of his cousins once for all."
He knew full well that his letter would shock his Union-
ist relatives, as indeed it did. This was his first small
act of rebellion against a world he dimly perceived as
complacent and materialistic.

When Stuart left Rugby in the summer of 1918 and returned to Ireland, he expected that his formal education was at an end. His mother, however, suddenly decided he should begin preparing for the entrance examinations required by Trinity College, Dublin. Consequently, in the autumn of 1918 he took a flat on the edge of the city with his mother, whose husband had by this time left her, after losing a considerable portion of her money on the stock exchange. Stuart, who was already interested in becoming a poet, had no real desire to enter Trinity or any other university. After about six months the whole venture was given up, without Stuart having so much as attempted the examinations. His mother then returned to the north early in 1919, and he was permitted to stay on in Dublin alone.

One event of some significance did occur during the winter of 1918. Mr. H.O. White, a fellow of Trinity College who had been engaged to tutor Stuart for the Trinity entrance examinations, invited Stuart and his Aunt Janet to accompany him to one of AE's Sunday evenings. Stuart vividly re-creates the visit in *Black List*. He remembers the walls of Russell's room lined with paintings in "misty blues and luminous shades of gray, depicting a dream landscape" which seemed to him entirely "false and invented." But what bothered him most was seeing the famous poet with his shaggy hair sitting before the small group and, with great satisfaction, reading aloud from press notices of his lecture tour in the United States, even passing around photographs of the large crowds that had greeted him in such cities as Boston and Philadelphia. In spite of the disillusionment Stuart experienced on this occasion, the gathering had one unexpected pleasure, for later that evening Iseult Gonne, Maud Gonne's strikingly beautiful daughter, joined the group. Although he and Iseult were not formally introduced that evening, their relationship had its beginning.

Mr. White had arranged for him to stay with Mrs. Travers Smith, whose daughter would later marry Lennox Robinson. For the first time he was on his own and felt free. The literary atmosphere, however, was not altogether to his liking. The books Mrs. Travers Smith suggested he read—books by Zola and Henry James, for instance—Stuart found difficult to get through, and her intellectual friends, who talked mostly of art, had little in common with him.

It was a young English medical student, Robert Fawcett, who did not talk "esoterically of books and pictures," who offered to take him to one of Maud Gonne's Tuesdays at home. Stuart remembers that he was at first reluctant, "feeling no inclination to leave the seclusion of his retreat in spite of the haunting memory of the girl who had turned out to be Iseult." In the end, though, he went to the house on St. Stephen's Green. He recalls that it was Iseult, a "tall girl in a sky-blue dress with a tasseled shawl," who met them in a first-floor room. Later Maud Gonne made her appearance dressed in black, and his reaction to "her single-minded obliviousness, and especially her effu-siveness," was instantly negative. Although for Stuart the whole affair was very uncomfortable, he left feeling that somehow a bond between Iseult and him had been established. Still, he realized that any chance for a seri-ous relationship between them was very unlikely. After all, he was only seventeen and she was twenty-three. She had lived in France, had moved in artistic circles there and later in England, had known W. B. Yeats and Ezra Pound intimately, and had a mother immortalized by Yeats as his Helen and Phoenix.

Not long after this meeting he and a young English staff officer, whom Stuart had met at Mrs. Travers Smith's, decided to make a walking trip to visit the Gonnes at their newly acquired cottage in Glenmalure, County Wicklow. Once there, Stuart's earlier impression of Maud Gonne was soon intensified almost to the point of hostility. The next day Stuart fared better. He took Iseult for a walk and gave her the copy of Yeats's poetry he had brought with him. Among the boulders that filled the top of the pass in the shadowy, narrow glen, he asked her to read one of the poems: "Iseult was only too ready to play the part he'd assigned her; he'd made a false move right at the start. He had placed his beloved in an unreal, Yeatsian world, instead of trying to take her into his which, however immature, was a very different one." That spring day the relationship, wrapped in romantic illusion, began to deepen. Within months they had more or less drifted into the decision to marry. Realizing that her mother would not look favorably on such a union, Iseult suggested that they go separately to London and meet there. In January 1920 they left Ireland and took a flat above a grocer's shop on Tottenham Street, a narrow lane just off London's Tottenham Court Road, where they lived for about three months without marrying.

Precisely how much Stuart knew at this time about Iseult's early life and family background is difficult to say, but it is likely that many of the details were revealed for the first time in the intimacy of their London flat. He probably did know beforehand that Iseult was not really Maud Gonne's adopted daughter, although she was so represented. H. O. White had told him after the evening at George Russell's that he thought the relationship was "a little closer than that, though it wouldn't do for Madame to admit it in the nationalist circles in which she moves." Iseult was in fact the natural daughter of Maud Gonne and Lucien Millevoye. A French deputy and noted orator, Millevoye had been associated with the Boulangists, a political faction that was strongly anti-Dreyfusard, opposed to the French parliamentary republic and to the *entente cordiale* between England and France. "Apparently they had some slight interest in the Irish question," Stuart recalls, "in fact, probably in anything that would be anti-English. And therefore Maud Gonne's interest in Millevoye was largely, I imagine now, political or nationalist . . . ." Iseult grew up in the politically charged atmosphere of her mother's world, tempered perhaps by the relative calm of the convent school where she was educated. She later came to know the art circles of Paris at firsthand and, through W. B. Yeats, had access to London's fashionable society, where she was the center of attention and the recipient of several marriage proposals.

In the shadow of Iseult's rich experiences, it is not surprising that Stuart began to wonder in the months spent in London why she had selected him over the others. His feelings are captured in *Black List:* "H didn't ask her why she had chosen a boy like himself with nothing to recommend him, immersed in his separate dream, idle, negatively disposed toward her mother (and to much else besides that she held in esteem, though this might yet not be apparent), poor, whose father had died of delirium tremens and whose own mental capabilities had been seriously questioned by most of the masters at his various schools." For Stuart the question would never really be answered, but one may assume that his own physical attractiveness had at least something to do with her choice: tall and slender, with eyes that seemed to retain the almost mystical depth and calm of the days at Shallon, he made a striking impression. Victor Gollancz, the publisher of many of Stuart's books and one of his most steadfast proponents, once said that he "was the handsomest man" he had ever met. Regardless of her reasons Iseult did choose him, though the decision would prove unfortunate for them both, because they really had too little in common to sustain a happy relationship.

During the latter part of their stay in London, Iseult became more and more concerned over letters she had been receiving from Helena Moloney, a friend of her mother's, urging them to come back to Ireland and indicating that Maud Gonne thought it prudent for them to be married. As a result, they did return to Dublin in early April. After Stuart had obtained his mother's consent to the marriage, he began receiving Catholic instruction, which he saw as little more than a formality. Once again he proved a recalcitrant student, objecting this time to "the sort of teaching that treated religion as a cut-and-dried subject." Nonetheless he completed instruction, and that same month married Iseult in University Church, only a few doors away from Maud Gonne's house on the Green.

In the summer of 1920, while Black-and-Tan lorries

rolled through the streets of Dublin, Iseult announced that she was pregnant. To Stuart, who was only eighteen, the news must have come as something less than a blessing. He already felt oppressed by Maud Gonne, who seemed to retain her hold on Iseult; he was frequently at odds with his wife over such issues as the Catholic Church and Irish nationalism as well as more personal matters; and now he had another responsibility which could only aggravate their already difficult financial situation. Some of his uneasiness is recorded in *Black List* : "It seemed to H they were being hemmed in on all sides, by his mother-in-law and her wide circle of admiring acquaintances (one of whom . . . lived in the same house and, he imagined, made her reports), by the curfew lately imposed on the city, and by some of their own habits such as the card playing and Iseult's general neglect of the flat, which he occasionally tried to straighten out in her absence."

By the end of the year they had fallen several months behind with their rent. In order to find the necessary money, they decided to sell the Montgomery necklace that Iseult had received as a wedding gift. Anticipating a better price for the jewelry in England than in Ireland, Stuart left for London early in January 1921 to see about the sale, while Iseult went to stay with her mother. The trip was in reality more of an escape than a business venture, for after quickly disposing of the necklace and sending back most of the money to Iseult, Stuart took a furnished room on Charlotte Street (not far from the Tottenham Street flat they had shared), where he stayed for nearly two months.

Within days of his arrival he became infatuated with

the beautiful Russian ballerina Tamara Karsavina, whom he saw perform at the Coliseum, on St. Martin's Lane. His reaction to her dancing was profound: "The disciplined rhythm imposed on the uprush of sensuous magic seemed familiar to him, the poetry of Keats, Shelley, and the later Yeats, made flesh." He returned to his room after the performance and completed two poems, which he sent to her the next day. In one of them "For a Dancer, I" he wrote of her "inaccessible beauty," which had left an "image on my maddened flesh/Like a white rose upon a thunderous sea." Although the poems resulted in his being invited backstage on several occasions, the liaison he had hoped for did not really develop, largely because of his self-consciousness about having so little money and his consequent lack of initiative. Perhaps the most significant thing about his feelings for the woman, and indeed about the entire period of his stay in London, is that it reveals how extremely fragile the union with Iseult actually was after less than a year of marriage; this separation was the first of many.

In March 1921, not long after he had returned to Dublin, Iseult gave birth to a daughter, Dolores. Stuart took virtually no interest in the child, even refusing to attend her christening in order to antagonize his mother-in-law. His lack of concern for the baby and his refusal to attend the ceremony were things he would come to regret deeply, for the girl soon developed spinal meningitis and died that July. It would be wrong to assume that the death had any very strong impact on him at the time; quite the contrary, he felt little guilt and showed little compassion for Iseult's pain. Over the years, though, the event took on great significance, at once per-

sonal and symbolic, as Stuart reveals in a letter written a half-century later:

> It is the ignominious or obscure deaths of the victims, the
> vulnerable, among whom I see both my father and my baby
> daughter, that I try to—I won't say atone for—but celebrate
> in my work as the kind of events that are of vital significance
> in man's inner development. . . . One of the tasks of the
> imaginative novelist is, through comparable, though less
> intense, experience, to see life through the pure eye of the
> losers.

One finds it difficult not to see a connection between
the death of the baby girl and the strong emphasis in
many of his novels on disease or deformity, particularly
when most of those afflicted are young girls or women.

Because of the difficulty Iseult had in adjusting to
the loss, Maud Gonne suggested that the three of them
go abroad to attend a performance of Wagner at the
newly built Munich opera house. The proposal was
quickly agreed to, and they set out in late August. As
it turned out, Munich was only the first stop on a long
continental trip. Although Maud Gonne did not accompany them any farther than Munich, Iseult and Stuart
went on to Nuremberg, Dresden, Prague, and finally
Vienna, where they spent the largest part of the six
months they were away from Ireland.

For Stuart, at least part of the journey held out a special attraction that had little to do with raising Iseult's
spirits. In Munich he saw a notice of a performance by
Miss Karsavina and wrote to her suggesting a meeting.
The two did indeed meet there, though again nothing
much happened beyond their having lunch together.

She was once more the inspiration for several poems—one "The Propylaen, Munich," named for the arch where they met, and another titled "Excuse," expressing both his sense of futility and his desire. The quest was extended to Prague when she told him she would be dancing there next, but again he was frustrated, forced to settle for another backstage visit. His hapless efforts ended in Prague with Tamara remaining the romantic image of unattainable beauty.

On June 28, 1922, only a short time after Stuart and his wife had returned to Ireland, Free State troops began shelling the Republican rebels in the Four Courts and Civil War flared. Maud Gonne's house on Stephen's Green was quickly turned into a makeshift hospital for Republican wounded. It was here that Stuart was drawn into the war, at first being assigned such menial tasks as carrying out slop pails, bringing up food trays, and occasionally applying simple dressings. His involvement, however, soon increased. At the request of one of the wounded I.R.A. leaders, he went to Belgium by way of Hull and Ostend and, perhaps as much to his surprise as anyone else's, succeeded in smuggling several guns back into Ireland. He was then sent to the south as a courier and was involved in several minor skirmishes. That August, after he had returned to Dublin, he joined in an ill-advised attempt by a small group of I.R.A. members, including some from the Dublin Brigade, to steal an armored car that regularly escorted Free State military vehicles to the Amiens Street railway station. While waiting at his position inside the station and listening to the rattle of gunfire outside, he was captured by two Free State soldiers and taken to Welling-

ton barracks before finally being interned in Marybor-
ough military prison and later in a camp at the Cur-
ragh, where he remained until November 1923.

Stuart's attitude toward the Civil War was curiously
mixed. He never became an official member of the Irish
Republican Army, though he participated in some of
its activities and carried a membership card for purposes
of identification. Initially he felt a certain enthusiasm
for the Republican cause, primarily because it was
something he could share with Iseult and even his
mother-in-law. For one of the few times in his life he
felt part of "a community of like-minded people," but
the enthusiasm was short-lived. He was not deeply
concerned with broad and impersonal political issues.
What he wanted was a freer society, less dogmatic and
more imaginative—one in which the artist could breathe
more easily. In too many of the Republican leaders he
sensed a basically reactionary nature. These men were
not the ones to lead the revolution Stuart had in mind.
Consequently, by the time of his capture he was quite
ready to be done with the war.

Arrangements for the private publication of his first
book were made during the last months of imprisonment
by a friend of his, the poet F. R. Higgins. The slim,
cheaply printed volume, dated 1923, though actually
appearing in January 1924, only two months after
Stuart's release, contained poems written between 1919
and August 1923, some of which had been published
earlier in *Poetry* and *The Chapbook*. Given Stuart's
alignment with the Republicans during the Civil War,
one is tempted to find political overtones in the title
We Have Kept the Faith, but the book is in fact free

of political motives and the title comes from Rupert Brooke's poem "The Hill." There is good reason to believe that the faith Stuart had in mind, aside from his faith in life itself, was a total commitment to the imagination, to art—to Blake and Coleridge and especially Keats—rather than to the cause of Arthur Griffith or Eamon de Valera.

One finds it easy enough today in leafing through the brown-edged pages to criticize much of the poetry as derivative, strained, and lacking in craftsmanship. It is easy, for instance, to question the poetic value of a line like "Drift southward, meward, loveward, to the sea!" from "Opium River." Indeed examples of weaknesses are all too plentiful. Still in nearly all of the poems one feels the poet's authentic effort to transform his own emotions into art. Moreover, to judge the book harshly is to forget that a number of the pieces were written when Stuart was only seventeen years old and that the latest one was written when he had just turned twenty-one.

Although the poems are in essence youthful experiments, they do occasionally touch on themes that will recur throughout his work. In "Bull Fight" Stuart explores the strange, primal attraction of violence. There is something erotic and mystical in his description of the dark, formally dressed ladies watching pitilessly as a bull's "dripping horn" tears at the still living flesh of a fallen horse. They are moved sensually until they, too, "Seem violent with breast and arm and thigh,/ Envious of the sand that drinks up death." "Criminals," written in 1919, combines the themes of the outcast and violence, as well as introducing for the first time a major

paradox in Stuart's work: the association of the erotic
with the religious. In this instance a man kills his beloved because he loves too passionately, and he in turn is
executed by society, but not before he has carved these
lines in the church the girl's mother attends: "I tied her
to a cross, and on the third day/She descended into
Hell, but she shall rise/To the sea's edge again and rot
away." The crucifixion and resurrection are here clearly parodied, but in several of the early novels the connection between a woman and a saint or even Christ is far
from parody.

Aside from such thematic foreshadowing, perhaps
the principal value of the work lies in what it reveals
about Stuart's artistic preferences, which have remained
unusually constant throughout his career. There is no
mistaking the romantic temper pervading the book:
one need only note the traditional romantic influences,
ranging from Blake to Keats, to be certain of that. The
implicit anti-intellectualism and the emphasis on passion,
individualism, spontaneity, and mysticism clearly define
both his earlier and later positions.

Shortly after its publication the book had the unexpected good fortune of coming to the attention of
W.B. Yeats, who evidently felt a certain kinship with
its author. Stuart himself was surprised by the interest
expressed by the man he had heard Iseult talk about so
much and whose works he had read and admired at
Rugby. In a memoir written many years later, Stuart
recalls the first meeting between the two writers and
"the shock" of hearing "this strange and rather chilling
figure with his eagle glance" discuss his first important
literary effort. Yeats, however, did more than merely

discuss the book; he announced that the Royal Irish Academy had decided to award it a prize.

While Stuart appreciated the generosity of the man, he never felt at ease (either on this occasion or the many others to follow) with Yeats's studied formality and humor, and he usually found it difficult to carry on a conversation with him—so much so that about five years later Yeats wrote a letter to Lady Gregory in which he said, doubtless with some exaggeration, that Stuart "is silent unless one brings the conversation round to St. John of the Cross or a kindred theme." Nonetheless, for more than a decade Yeats remained his most prestigious advocate.

He was in fact to prove helpful again only a few months after the first meeting when Stuart, together with F.R. Higgins, Cecil Salkeld, and Con Leventhal, proposed bringing out a new periodical to be called *To-Morrow*. Yeats's dream of having "a wild paper of the young which will make enemies everywhere & suffer suppression & hate a number of times" had at least partial fulfillment when the first number finally appeared in August 1924. The issue contained an editorial written by Yeats (but appearing over the names of Stuart and Salkeld) in which he lashed out against cultural standards in Irish society and in the Irish Catholic Church. Yeats also supplied a poem, "Leda and the Swan," published that June in *The Dial*, which was controversial in its own right. Stuart describes the impact the issue had in his memoir of Yeats:

> I don't think we realised what a bombshell we were exploding when we printed this article, to say nothing of the poem

with its strange, perverse eroticism. I know *I* didn't.
"To-Morrow," of which we had envisaged selling a very
limited number in Leventhal's bookshop, was soon sold
out. It was discussed and denounced, and was seen being
read in such unlikely places as the dining-room of a hotel
in Athlone and a country pub in Donegal. This delighted
Yeats, who loved controversy and pitting himself against
the less imaginative and daring.

The extraordinary success obviously delighted Stuart
as well, for anything that jarred conventional opinion
always strongly appealed to him. Unfortunately, the
notoriety generated by this first number was not enough
to sustain the journal very long. After the publication
of the second issue in September, *To-Morrow* col-
lapsed, and with it Yeats's dream.

Early in 1924 Stuart and Iseult took a cottage south
of Dublin in Glencree, County Wicklow. There were
still frequent visits to Dublin, but it was the relative
seclusion of the whitewashed cottage, with its reddish
iron roof and garden enclosed by a stone fence, that
really attracted Stuart. During the first two years he
found a peace that he had not experienced since leaving Shallon, and Iseult and he were probably happier
at this time than they ever would be again. Things
changed with the birth of their son Ian in 1926. Stuart
notes in his diary: "The last two years or so there after
Ian's birth were different. We were no longer alone, my
mother was there too and I turned more and more to
religion. But in a too violently mental way and the
result was terrible inner storm and revolution, though
moments of fulfillment."

At least at the beginning of this period, Stuart continued to see himself as essentially a poet and did contribute a poem to *To-Morrow*. Yet the impulse seemed to weaken during the next several years. He published two poems in *The Transatlantic Review* in October 1924, four in *Poetry* in November, one in *The Chapbook* in 1925, another in *The Dublin Magazine* in the summer of 1926, and then five more in *Poetry* in October 1926. After this, no more appeared. The "inner storm and revolution" evidently had taken their toll on his creative energy. Perhaps, too, he was beginning to have doubts about his future as a poet or at least about his ability to support a family by writing poetry.

While the years at Glencree were rather unproductive artistically, they were in any case extremely important, for they were years of extensive reading and contemplation, which helped lay the foundation for the novels that would begin appearing in 1931. After reading Evelyn Underhill's *Mysticism* in 1926, Stuart became deeply absorbed with the mystics, whose boundless imagination and emotion appealed to him and whose states of consciousness he recognized as being akin to his own. He read the lives of saints—among them, Catherine of Siena, Rose of Lima, Thérèse of Lisieux, and John of the Cross. In their passionate relationship to God he found the nexus between the erotic and religious, between this world and the other. He also studied the works of Blake, Jacob Boehme, and William Law, as well as the lives of Keats and Dostoevsky. Far more significant, however, was his reading of the Gospels, in which he found a paradigm for his theories about the outcast and, on another level, about the role of the artist in society. As he explained it in *Black List*, Christ was someone who had achieved "new kinds of perception and emotion" and who wished principally "to find and keep a few friends who were capable of sharing this new intensity." His failure to do so required a last, incredible effort through self-sacrifice. It is clear enough that this is a Christ who would not appeal to the hierarchy of the Catholic Church.

Yet, while at Glencree Stuart was as close to the Catholic Church as he would ever be. A number of his views would nevertheless have been considered heretical, if not blasphemous. He questioned the concept of Mary's bodily Assumption and felt that Christ's Resurrection was something of a mistake because it introduced a kind of "grocer's scheme of reward and punishment." Nor did he have much regard for the average priest. With all, he did attend Mass quite regularly for a time, walking nearly five miles each morning to the local church. He also erected a portable shed in his garden where he studied the mystics and in his own way lived an ascetic life. In 1928 he and Iseult went on a pilgrimage to Lourdes, and in spite of the tawdriness and commercialism of the place, Stuart was genuinely moved by the story of the Blessed Bernadette and by the grotto in which she had had her vision of the Virgin Mary. He even went so far as to become a brancardier in order to attend the crippled and sick who came to the shrine.

Though his religious feelings were entirely authentic and nearly all of his later books might be described as in some sense religious, it is ironic that he has been routinely classified as a "Catholic" author. If he is Catholic, it is only in the broadest theological sense. In a letter to this writer, he commented on the relationship between his work and Catholicism: "My novels are certainly not 'Catholic' novels. That is not to say that I have completely rejected the Catholic Church as have almost all serious Irish writers. As the hero of my last novel says: 'My psyche is *au fond* a believing, not a sceptical one.'"

2

Images of Eternity

Early in 1929, Stuart and his wife purchased a thick-walled granite structure built by the British at the end of the eighteenth century and subsequently modified to look like a medieval castle. Located at the southeastern end of the beautiful Vale of Glendalough in County Wicklow, well back from the main road and partially hidden by trees, Laragh Castle afforded even greater seclusion than their previous home in Glencree and had the further attraction for someone fascinated by the mystics of being only a few miles away from the ruins of the ancient monastic colony founded by Kevin in the sixth century. Outwardly, at least, it was the ideal place for someone of Stuart's introspective and mystical temperament, but the peace it offered was more than offset by his inner struggles.

At Laragh, really for the first time, he and his family were financially on their own. Maud Gonne had supplied the money for the purchase of the new home, and up to this time they had been more or less dependent on a small, often irregular allowance from Stuart's mother. Now, however, there was acute pressure to find a way to meet at least ordinary expenses. Perhaps hoping to demonstrate some of the same ingenuity that had made his father and uncles prosperous sheep ranchers in Australia, Stuart set about raising poultry. He was in fact moderately successful, though not so successful that money ceased to be a problem.

The years Stuart spent here from 1929 to 1939 reflect all too clearly his own instability, marked by violent psychic swings between the desire for isolation and the desire to immerse himself in the world. He believed life should be lived *in extremis*. Laragh was at best only a partial refuge. Although he found pleasure in his son Ian and his daughter Katherine, born in 1931, his relationship with Iseult became even more abrasive and tense over the years, and he spent long periods away from home. In the early thirties he made a second visit to Lourdes, this time without Iseult, and he later participated in a retreat lasting about two weeks in the Cistercian Abbey at Roscrea. On other occasions he spent a month or more alone in Dublin or with his friend Liam O'Flaherty at his flat in London. During the stays in Dublin and London there were bouts of heavy drinking and involvements with a number of women—at least one of these affairs was serious enough for him to consider trying to divorce Iseult. In his Berlin diary of 1942 he recreates the turbulence of the period with startling candor; even the rushed, choppy style, which is quite uncharacteristic of the diary as a whole, reveals the deep intensity of his struggle:

> Then Laragh. The poultry. Lack of money that was acute . . . for the next nine or ten years.
> Beginning to write novels. Their failure as far as money

was concerned. Tormented foolishly because of this. Working too much. Too isolated and the reaction of hectic plunging into the world. The mad vain search for fulfillment through such people as Paulina, Christabel, Honor, Ethel, Avia, Margery, Ruth, Beattie . . . , and even more futile, because emotionless, episodes like Nell, Emily and one or two others.

Racing, Sunnymova and Galamac [horses he owned]. Trying to find fulfillment in the excitement of that and in the mad hope of large winnings. Drink too.

It was perhaps only in the act of writing that he found a measure of self-fulfillment at Laragh, sitting alone in "a small bare room with grey walls and a deal floor and a window looking on to a mountain." In this stark, cloistral setting he could free his imagination and create fictional worlds that reflected his own search for meaning and stability. Yet the novels, while no doubt cathartic on the personal level, actually explore deeper levels of reality and set the insights revealed against the sterility of a society, of a civilization, from which he had long felt alienated.

Apart from his own lived experience, the source of these early works, which seemed to burst from a store of creative energy, lay in his earlier reading of the mystics and particularly the Gospels. Many years later Stuart wrote that the philosophy, to the extent it could be called a philosophy, "derives, I think, above all from the Gospels, if from the Gospels interpreted in a personal manner. It is an instinctive belief in pain, ignominy and defeat as vital in expanding and developing the consciousness. The life of Christ . . . was my original guide in this."

Significantly, the crucifixion, if taken broadly enough to include the loneliness and agony man passes through, is the central recurring symbol in his work. In essence this is a tragic vision not unlike that of the Greek dramatists, who saw tragedy in terms of the hero stripped of all tangible supports, wandering in uncharted regions, suffering in his loneliness before attaining self-knowledge and knowledge of the power of the gods. For Stuart the pattern was much the same, only the God was different. Pain and humiliation were necessary to turn man away from the appearances of the world and to force him to look inward; for like the blind Oedipus, only then could he truly see.

His first novel, *Women and God*, which appeared in 1931, is by nearly any standard unsuccessful. Stuart seemed compelled to pour into it all his attitudes toward love, religion, and society without much regard to how he was going to embody them in character and action. As a consequence, there is a mad rush of ideas, which too often appear detached and abstract. This, along with dialogue that often seems forced and the generally uneven quality of the writing, does not make the book a very auspicious beginning.

One of his main problems was that he had not found a style or a form in which he could work. Unfortunately, he chose as a model Hemingway's *The Sun Also Rises,* a fine book of its kind but not one that proved very amenable to what Stuart wanted to do. For one thing, Hemingway's style, with its short, simple sentences that work through ironic understatement, was not natural to Stuart, whose tendency at this time was more toward the lyrical, even sentimental: "The thing that love is so floods our little beings that we want to take all the life that is coming to us and throw it before our lover. And that's not enough. Nothing is enough. O God! It's torture. It's sweet! It's terrible!" Aside from this fault, and others even more serious, like the absence of a clear narrative focus, the novel does have a value because it contains in embryonic form several elements that will be more expertly handled in later works. *Women and God* is essentially an attempt to trace man's search for meaning in a world that seems profoundly dark and empty. Using a series of characters that would, for the most part, fit into Hemingway's world of the lost generation, Stuart reveals the vanity of trying to find meaning in purely physical love, in science, or in the excitement of automobile racing or horse racing. Ultimate meaning exists only in the awareness of God's presence.

Because the novel grew out of Stuart's relationship with Iseult and his own experiences in Lourdes and Paris and was based on a number of people he had actually known, its failure came as a disheartening blow. "I found and opened the reviews," Stuart wrote in *Things to Live For*. "Few novels can have had such shockingly bad ones. I had craved for success. It was a knock all right." What he refused to accept at the time was that the book deserved the reviews it received. That he nevertheless did learn from what he had done is borne out by his second novel, *Pigeon Irish,* published the following year, which in terms of sales and critical reception proved to be the most successful book he ever wrote. Yeats praised it; Compton Mackenzie praised it; and it was featured on the front page of the

New York Times Book Review section. The acclaim he had wanted, he received many times over.

Although *Pigeon Irish* does not mark any startling philosophical departure from his first novel, it does show a major technical advance. Stuart avoids the wavering narrative focus of the previous book, keeps his four major characters under firm control, and maintains a consistent tone. Moreover, probably because of his earlier reading of mystical literature, he moves strongly in the direction of symbolism, verging frequently on allegory. Within this form, which is essentially that of the modern parable or fable, he is able to suggest effectively those deeper layers of experience and consciousness which had long been his principal interest.

Two views of life, the scientific and the mystical, provide the basic frame for *Pigeon Irish*. Stuart sets the story in Ireland at an indefinite time in the future when a war is raging on the continent of Europe. The contending forces are purely allegorical. On one side is an army, now threatening to sweep over Ireland, that represents a super-civilization, materialistic and scientific, and that aims at complete domination: "Science controlling life. Hygiene. Hygienic love. A psychotherapic religion." On the other side is a beleaguered army, which is virtually all that remains of a civilization based on the blend of the physical and spiritual that Stuart saw as peculiarly Irish.

The central line of action describes the psychic journey of Frank Allen, the narrator of the story. Frank, who reluctantly assumes command of the Irish Home Guard in the absence of his friend Joe Arigho, accepts the premise that the only way to save what is essentially Irish is to give up Dublin to the enemy and set up secret colonies in "areas in certain parts of the country where those best fitted to carry on the old way of life, to keep our values, faith and so on, would live, holding the last outposts in Europe." When this plan is presented to the army high command, it is considered treasonous, and not long afterward General Frank Allen is arrested and summarily condemned to death. Only the return of Joe, who steps in and allows himself to be shot in his place, prevents the execution. Frank, however, goes through his own form of crucifixion when he is intentionally misrepresented in the army's account of the incident as having knowingly allowed Joe to die for him. He is made an outcast in his own country, even losing his wife, Brigid, to another man. Only Catherine, Joe's daughter, stays to comfort him, and it is she who expresses Frank's position most clearly: "I thought you had to die for Ireland. I thought that two days ago. Now I see that it isn't an outward death. It's a martyrdom. An inner stripping bare." Yet, in spite of the defeat and degradation, both Catherine and Frank remain to uphold and perpetuate the traditional values in a world that is crumbling about them.

Within the broad allegorical frame there are a number of complex symbolic dimensions. Employing the ancient genre of the fable and a highly lyrical style, the author interweaves a narrative of three pigeons with the more realistic, Hemingwayesque chapters. On the surface, at least, the pigeons, raised by Catherine, are simply used to carry messages to and from the troops at the battlefront. Metaphorically, however, the birds become a modern equivalent of the raven and the dove sent out from the ark to discover if the flood has receded, though in this case the waters never abate and the true population of the ark is eventually reduced to Catherine and Frank. And finally the pigeons symbolize the spirit of Ireland—the oneness of the physical and spiritual—and it is no coincidence that the number-one pigeon base is located in the monastic ruins at Glendalough.

Free of the artificial barriers erected by civilization, the pigeons have a completely harmonious relationship because it is unconscious and emotional. The female pigeon most deeply aware of her ties with the raven and dove corresponds to Catherine, whose patron saint is Catherine of Siena, the adviser to popes and politicians; and the other female, more sensuous than spiritual, suggests Brigid, Frank's wife. The male bird, on the other hand, is related to two characters: Joe, whose "slate-grey uniform with red bands" obviously resembles the "slate-grey cock pigeon" with coral legs, and Frank Allen, who wears an identical uniform when he assumes command. Yet, among the humans the relationship falls short of perfection, as suggested by Brigid's jealousy of Catherine. Clearly the ideal mystical union no longer existed in Ireland. Stuart reinforces the point by emphasizing the strong antagonism between the army command, which opposes Joe and Frank, and the air force command, which supports them: symbolically the two forces reflect the physical and spiritual.

Stuart's portrait of modern Ireland is darkly pessimistic, no doubt because of his own disillusionment with the Free State government. What hope there is lies in those, like Frank and Catherine, who refuse to give up their burning vision. That they at least will find redemption is prefigured in the final chapter, when Conquistador, the male pigeon that dies after carrying out its mission, is symbolically lifted heavenward by the gentle fingers of Archangels. Whether Ireland will find salvation is left much less certain.

Pigeon Irish is probably Stuart's most ambitious pre-war novel and certainly one of the most important. This is not to say that the book is free of faults. The pigeon subplot, for instance, in spite of its symbolic function (or perhaps because of it), seems needlessly contrived and consequently never really merges with the main line of action except in a rather mechanical fashion. Furthermore, Stuart's failure to make the language and situations in the subplot always convincing seriously weakens the book as a whole. Still, even with its defects, the novel marks a very important advance in his work, largely because it gives clear expression to the value of suffering and sacrifice in drawing one to the ideal, and establishes for the first time the theme of victory in defeat, which will recur in all of the major works.

His third novel, *The Coloured Dome*, published in July 1932, a scant five months after *Pigeon Irish*, takes up the underlying theme of the previous work and further refines it. The narrative centers on an ordinary turf accountant Garry Delea, whose life in Dublin has been dreary and pointless. He is asked by Tulloolagh to join her and two other Republican leaders in sacrificing themselves so that a large number of minor Republicans might live. Garry eagerly accepts the offer and finds happiness in the belief that he has cast off all vestiges of self, a belief that is really nothing more than another form of pride. When by chance he and Tulloolagh are not executed, he is forced to reexamine his position. What he discovers is that he has only begun the process of stripping away the self. His spirit has merely passed through its spring and must still move through summer and autumn before finding peace in winter. He achieves this peace later, after he gives himself up at Mountjoy prison and is thrown into a cell filled with the sour, sickening smell of wet bodies. "Only thus could he begin to share the vulgar, sordid and sometimes ludicrous suffering of the world."

Stuart unifies the work by building it around an image borrowed from the famous passage in Shelley's "Adonais": "Life, like a dome of many-coloured glass, /Stains the white radiance of Eternity." Allusions to the simile range from a street trader's trinket that falls to the concrete and shatters into "curved pieces of coloured glass" to the crescent shape of cobblestones. Garry's inner task is to discover the key to the colored fragments. He finds it when he at last undergoes the mystical experience of the death of the self: "A white radiance fell through his consciousness unstained by that coloured dome. As though life had become simple with the translucence of eternity." The book ends with Garry still in his cell, his fate undecided; but whether he is executed or not has now become incidental even to him. He has already experienced death and found the mystical still point.

With *Pigeon Irish* and *The Coloured Dome,* Stuart

had reached the peak of his early career, and from 1933 through 1939 there is a general, though uneven, decline in quality. The spiritual intensity that provided the energy for his two best books seems to glow only intermittently afterward. His first three novels had been published during a brief ten-month period. Between January 1933 and October 1934, four more works appeared—two novels, a play, and an autobiography. Driven by the pressing need for money, which was due in part to his own incontinence, he was writing at a feverish pace.

One senses, however, that there was more involved in the decline than merely his writing too much. Indeed, the evidence would appear to indicate that he had not been able to satisfy his desire for some kind of durable spiritual peace. Perhaps the most telling sign of this is the artificial quality that mars even the best of the early works. In a note in his Berlin diary, Stuart himself shows an awareness of what had happened: "When I began to write . . . 'Women and God' there was a religious obsession but it was and had been too mental and I was already escaping from it and turning to the world for adventure and inspiration." As he turned to the world, if mainly for the purpose of attacking its materialism and skepticism, he drifted farther and farther from the source of his strength.

Neither *Try the Sky* nor *Glory,* the two novels that appeared in 1933, is as satisfying artistically as those of the previous year. Although there is no substantial philosophical or technical departure from the earlier books, signs of strain are much more in evidence. The quality of the writing is noticeably lower, particularly in *Try the Sky,* where it is possible to find such uncon-

vincing passages as this: "O Ireland! O Carlotta! O
Love! I thought passionately. What little, little faith
I have. Oh, yes, it is true; this is heaven. You are my
heaven, you three together!" And still another indication that he is beginning to falter is his tendency in both
books to assemble almost surrealistic groups of characters, as though he were struggling to be as unconvention-
al and shocking as possible for no very good reason.
In *Glory* there are, among others, a Russian prince,
an English general, a Chinese warlord, and an Irish
ascetic.

Like *Pigeon Irish*, *Try the Sky* is very much concerned
with the seeming dichotomy between the physical and
spiritual impulses in man, only this time treating the
two principles as they relate to human love. The first
part, "The Abyss," focuses mainly on the earthly view,
as symbolized by the Danube (which bears more than
a casual relationship to Blake's River of Life) and by
Buttercup, the American Indian who models plaster
casts of an archetypal river and who remarks to José
on one occasion: "I try to live wrapped in the spirit
of nature or life or the earth, whatever you call it. I
don't think so many thoughts as you . . . . " In her
primitive, prerational quality, Buttercup closely resembles the pigeons in *Pigeon Irish*, one of which has
the same name. The second part of the book, "The
Flight," is clearly intended to balance the first by centering on the flight of a mysterious airplane named *The
Spirit,* symbolic of the soaring, romantic, lyrical love
between José and Carlotta that tries to escape the earth.
Here, as in *Pigeon Irish* and later in *Glory,* images
of flight are closely associated with spiritual illumina-

tion. That the plane in this case makes it only from Munich to a desolate area in Ireland is not really so depressing as it might seem, for the ideal is a merging of the earthly and spiritual. Although José is initially disappointed, even he comes to understand that what he and Carlotta have found is a spiritualized love that cannot, that should not, be separated from the painful reality of the physical world.

Glory represents one of Stuart's more vitriolic expressions of dissatisfaction with modern society. In *Pigeon Irish* the author had embodied the threat of materialism, mechanization, and science in the army that stands poised to sweep over Ireland. In *Glory* the threat is even more immediate. The building of an aerodrome by Trans-Continental Aero-routes on the west coast of Ireland, the last stronghold of traditional Irish values, signals the actual presence of the hostile force. Frank de Lacy, a deeply religious man whose hermitage lies only a short distance from the oppressive concrete runways, senses the destructive nature of those who control the company: "Their mechanical obsession is overshadowing the whole of life. Even human love is becoming a sort of mechanical relationship." What little hope there is lies in those few who reject the dehumanizing philosophy and become society's outcasts.

While there were signs of diminished energy in *Try the Sky* and *Glory,* it is not until the publication of *In Search of Love* that one can see a sharp veering away from the course he had established in the earlier books. In a letter to Joseph O'Neill, dated August 30, 1935, Stuart wrote: "My own novel is out—not a serious one though, just a joke which I hope comes off." Un-

happily, the joke does not. Written in a month and a
half—and showing it in style and conception—*In
Search of Love* is his first, and last, venture into satire,
a form that does not seem even remotely congenial
to him. The purpose of the novel, in spite of his dis-
claimer, is entirely serious. Outwardly, the work is a
pointed attack on the commercialism of the film industry
and the gullibility of the public. Stuart indeed had had
some experience with motion pictures through his friend
Brian Desmond Hurst, a London filmmaker. In the
book, however, the industry is more a symptom of
the disease of twentieth-century commercialism and
materialism than the disease itself.

To a certain extent, Stuart recovered his power in
The Angel of Pity, which appeared near the end of 1935.
The book may have been inspired in part by Joseph
O'Neill's novel *Day of Wrath*. He had written O'Neill in
April of that year: "It never seems to have occurred to
anyone else to write a book about the next war in its
effect on the civilian population as you have done.
These good ideas seem so obvious *once someone has hit
on them.*" *The Angel of Pity* opens: "I imagine a grey
morning breaking over some desolate front in the next
great war. I am crouching in a concrete redoubt, partially
blown in, with one companion, the sole survivors of a
waste of mud and water reflecting the concrete-coloured
sky." For Stuart, though, the indefinite time and
place of the next war are used primarily as a backdrop
against which he projects his own philosophy. The
first-person narrator is unabashedly the author: "I
felt myself to be the last unsilenced voice, the only one
left to make a gesture of defiance. But I smiled to

myself at my own poor arrogance, as though a poet . . .
could stem the forward march of the new Progress."
The book, which owes at least something to the medieval passion play, takes the form of a spiritual journey leading the narrator to a deeper awareness of the
necessity of suffering and compassion. It is the young
girl Sonia who provides him with the necessary
instruction. She is the avatar of Christ as woman, and
her humiliation and murder at the hands of a group
of soldiers become the equivalent of Christ's passion
and death. The narrator, who witnesses this modern
version of the crucifixion, remembers her last words,
"Be compassionate." The effect of this experience on
him is profound; for the first time he is able to reach
out and grasp life, whether ugly or beautiful, and lavish
on it genuine love. Here in a plain left desolate by the
machinery of warfare, something indestructible had
blossomed.

Although Benedict Kiely wrote in *Modern Irish
Fiction* that *The Angel of Pity* "may yet come justly
to be regarded as his most notable book," this judg-
ment seems excessive. The novel certainly has its
virtues, not the least of which is the light it throws
on Stuart's philosophy, but it suffers from loose
construction and definite repetitiveness. Instead of al-
lowing the central fable to suggest his meaning, Stuart
frequently and disturbingly breaks away from the
story line in order to have his narrator record in a
notebook his unassimilated and abstract thoughts
about what is going on around him and about life in
general.

The four novels published after *The Angel of Pity*

are of generally lower quality than those that preceded it. Stuart seems to be writing as much out of a force of habit as out of any clearly defined conviction. The first of these books, *The White Hare*, which came out in 1936, is in some respects the most satisfying. Strands of the earlier lyricism are still to be found, and the symbolism is well-handled. Set in County Galway and Dublin, the novel describes the withering influence of modern bourgeois society on the romantic spirit. Dominic de Lacey and his older brother, Patrick, among the last of the old romantic aristocracy, are forced to leave the family's large, rather dilapidated country estate in the west of Ireland because of their continuing need for money. Patrick, the more tractable of the two, accepts a clerkship at Caldecott's Radiators in Dublin and takes his wife, the lovely and adventurous Hylla, and Dominic to live in the city. The tragic consequences are foreshadowed midway in the book when Dominic's greyhound scares up and kills the white hare that the boy had long dreamed of finding, "a symbol in his imagination of his own destiny," and "of Hylla ..., because his destiny was somehow bound up with her." The death of the hare is, however, more than just a symbol of Dominic's and Hylla's destiny. It is a symbol of the destruction of all that is wild and innocent and spiritual, the destruction of a way of life in the murderous jaws of a shopkeeper's society. Patrick, who acquiesces in his bleak existence, is soon pulled down into the empty routine of his job and becomes little more than a soulless husk. Submitting more reluctantly but no less inevitably, Hylla has the very life drawn from her, until her features resemble the dry, white bones of the hare's skeleton. And Dominic, rebelling by going off to sea, is drowned when his ship sinks during a violent storm. The defeat is total. No longer is there that flickering hope of redemption through sacrifice.

The next two novels convey much the same bitterness toward contemporary life. *The Bridge,* published the next year, exposes the drabness and puritanism of the ordinary Irish provincial town, Fert, and *Julie,* published in 1938, lashes out against London's impersonal, money-oriented society. *The Great Squire,* Stuart's last novel before the war, moves away from the unvarnished—and largely unsuccessful—social criticism of the three previous books and returns to the parabolic form of the earlier novels. Although marred by the gothic trappings that fill the opening chapter and by a number of improbable incidents, it does demonstrate that Stuart had never completely lost the vision informing such books as *Pigeon Irish* and *The Coloured Dome.*

The novel is set in late eighteenth-century Ireland at the time of the United Irishmen. The central character, Garrett O'Neil, is representative of the old order, believing "in nothing but in a way of life that was doomed, a dying feudalism." O'Neil can sympathize with the nationalist cause espoused by the United Irishmen but not with the French-inspired liberalism and egalitarianism that permeate it. The book, however, is less concerned with the clash of huge social forces than with O'Neil's search for personal meaning. The social prestige he initially wins, which results in the epithet The Great Squire, soon tastes of ashes, and he is led slowly and painfully to an awareness of suffering and to a renewed faith. The transcending love he discovers with Sue Melbourne and his newly found humility lead ultimately to a capacity for sacrifice. He has discovered mystical contentment and sheds the self altogether when he allows himself to be executed in place of his half-brother, who has been condemned to death for fighting on the side of the United Irishmen.

Shortly after *The Great Squire* appeared in February 1939, Stuart was approached by Helmut Clissmann, who was then head of the German Academic Exchange Service in Ireland, and invited to lecture and give readings from his novels in Germany under the sponsorship of Die Deutsche Akademie. He accepted the invitation, unaware of just how profoundly that decision would alter his life. At the moment, it must have seemed little more than an innocuous slap at the kind of respectability he despised. After all, a lecture tour lasting only a few months could hardly be construed as a firm ideological commitment to Nazism.

Stuart was conscious of the possibility of war when he left in April. (Only the month before, Germany had occupied portions of Czechoslovakia.) The world was tense that spring, but Stuart was willing to risk being caught in Germany should war break out. While in Berlin, he met Professor Hans Galinsky, a lecturer in the Englische Seminar at Berlin University, and Galinsky offered to talk to the director of his academic division, Professor Walter Schirmer, about arranging a faculty appointment for him. Stuart recalls: "I was never appointed at that time, but as I was rather short of money, Professor Schirmer arranged for me to give some lectures which were quite well paid." The director did indicate, though, that he would try to get him a formal appointment for the coming year. In July he returned to Ireland to await word.

Clearly Stuart's willingness to go to Germany at a time when most English and Irish writers would have refused, and his willingness, once there, to consider a formal teaching position, raise serious questions about his politics, questions that obviously cannot be ignored. It must be admitted that he held some views that would not have been alien to Fascism. For instance, he had written scathingly of democracy in *Things to Live For*: "Democracy is the ideal of those whose lives as individuals are failures and who, feeling their own futility, take refuge in the mass and become arrogant in the herd. The productive worker . . . does not believe in the rule of the majority because he does not feel himself to be one of the majority."

Yet the spirit of the man and his work is hardly Fascist. He was openly hostile to the suppression of personal freedom by any institution, whether governmental, religious, or social; indeed he had little use for institutions at all. Furthermore, he did not accept the insane racial doctrines promulgated by the National Socialists. There is no evidence whatever that he saw the Jew as part of an international conspiracy or as the incarnation of evil. Although he was not sympathetic to what he saw as the Jewish obsession with money, the Jew was, as the archetypal outcast, a natural ally and was treated as such in *Julie*. Stuart, moreover, was not attracted to Germany's imperialistic designs, having himself experienced the effects of English imperialism in Ireland. Nor is it at all likely that he accepted Na-

tional Socialist religious policies, which at one point
recommended for the proposed National Reich Church
that the cross be replaced by the swastika; the Bible
by *Mein Kampf;* and, in effect, Christ by der Führer.
It is not a Nazi who enters in his wartime diary, as
Stuart did: "God and the absence of god: the absence
of god is all deadness—the deadness of most institutions, sects, movements, parties. There is usually some
living spark in individuals." In a letter to this writer
in May 1971, Stuart spoke pointedly of Fascism:

> It has never seemed to me that anyone of imagination
> and psychic complexity could be a Fascist. To accuse
> somebody, a writer, who has, even to some degree,
> these characteristics is either malicious or stupid. At
> the same time there were certain very fine writers, Mon-
> therlant and Genet for instance, for whom Fascism was
> no more irrelevant, ridiculous (as a way-of-life) and
> criminal than the opposing ideologies and ways-of-life.
> The difference being that the latter had the added nas-
> tiness of self-righteousness.

Stuart's motives for going to Germany and for
wanting to stay there were highly complex. One might
point first of all to that strong impulse to do the shocking, which had long been apparent in him and which
probably grew out of the same self-destructive tendency
evident in his bouts of heavy drinking. Then, too, the
circumstances of his life no doubt played a crucial role
in his decision. His financial situation was precarious;
his career as a novelist was faltering badly; and his
marriage, unstable throughout the thirties, had reached
the intolerable state of mutual hostility. These pressures
alone must have made the comparative isolation of

Francis Stuart

Nazi Germany very attractive to him. But it would be wrong to view his personal problems as the only explanation for his actions. He had long felt that Western civilization was materialistic, decadent, and hostile to spiritual illumination. Only after the established order had been shaken to the ground did he foresee the possibility of constructing a new civilization more in keeping with his dreams. Hannah Arendt, writing in *Origins of Totalitarianism*, touches on the source of such feelings when she describes how members of the social elite, of whom the intellectuals formed a part, were attracted to totalitarianism, not because of their sympathy with a particular program, but because of "their desire to see the ruin of this whole world of fake security, fake culture, and fake life." There seems little doubt that, at the time, Stuart considered Hitler (as virtually the apotheosis of the outcast) the person most likely to accomplish the necessary destruction.

But in *Black List, Section H* Stuart remembers how his conception of Hitler began to change as a result of his lecture tour in Germany: "H was revising his original surmise about him as a blind and infuriated Samson about to pull down the whole pretentious edifice. Hitler had not the stature of Stalin who, like nearly all those dubbed as monsters by enlightened opinion, exerted a certain spell on H as, at least, the antithesis of the mediocrities in the public eye at home." Whatever illusions Stuart might still have maintained about Hitler's character and aims did not long survive. References to the German leader are significantly absent from his Berlin diary. Instead, one finds Stuart in

1942 castigating the Nazi Propaganda Ministry for having "no interest in nor knowledge of truth." Certainly by this time, if not before, he saw Hitler and his regime in proper perspective, but this is not to say that he considered the man worse than Churchill or Roosevelt, who represented a way of life he despised.

3

The Dark Night

Stuart received word from Professor Schirmer late in the summer of 1939 that a post as lecturer in modern English and Irish literature awaited him at Berlin University. In early January 1940, at last having gotten a passport containing no evidence of his previous trip to Germany, a certificate from a sympathetic doctor that he was tubercular, a twenty-four-hour transit visa through France, and an entry visa to Switzerland for health reasons, Stuart was able to begin his journey. As he walked through the arch in the thick stone walls enclosing Laragh Castle, he must have felt both expectation and foreboding. He was, to be sure, leaving behind him an unsatisfactory life, but he was also leaving the relative security of these walls for a life that offered no certainties at all.

Within days of his arrival in Berlin he moved into a flat on Westfälischestrasse and took up his teaching post in the Englische Seminar. It was not long before his involvement in German affairs deepened. He was approached by Dr. Schobert, a former lecturer in German at a Welch university, now connected with the German Foreign Office and concerned with propaganda broadcasts, and asked if he would be willing to write some talks for broadcast to England. Stuart agreed to the proposal, while sensing that the decision would damn him in the eyes of those who felt themselves right-thinking and respectable and, regardless of his motives, would carry with it the ineffaceable stigma of collaboration. He wrote in *Black List:* "In agreeing, H was turning from the busy street to slink with thieves and petty criminals down dim alleys, leaving the lawful company to which he'd belonged to become, in its eyes, a traitor." Far less consciously, Stuart was taking another step along the path of psychic exposure that he had described intuitively through the characters of Frank Allen and Garry Delea.

These initial talks were in fact few in number. He began writing them in April, and only six or eight were actually broadcast by William Joyce (Lord Haw Haw). The intent of the pieces, Stuart recalled in a letter to this writer, was "to express scepticism about the British moral attitude in waging the war [by] recalling some incidents in the history of British imperialism." He went on to say that "this . . . was not really what the Germans, or Joyce, wanted. They admired and envied British, or any other, imperialism." It was evidently for this reason that Stuart was not asked to continue writing. Instead, Joyce began composing his own copy, which was belligerently pro-Nazi.

Not long after Stuart started to write the talks, he was inadvertently caught up in some wartime intrigue that had serious repercussions. Captain Hermann Goertz, a German intelligence officer preparing for a secret mission to Ireland designed in part to establish contact with the I.R.A., made it a point to talk with Stuart and other Irishmen before leaving Germany. In a statement made to the Irish Secret Service after his eventual capture, Goertz said of Stuart: "He had nothing to do with the Abwehr [German Intelligence Service], he was no politician, he had no contacts with the I.R.A. and not much knowledge about them. But he was a genuine Irish patriot and the prototype of those people who later became my friends in Ireland." While it appears that Stuart had been of little practical use to Goertz, the matter did not end there. On the night of May 5, the German officer was dropped by parachute into Ireland. The Abwehr had given him the names of several places where he might secure aid in the event of an emergency—one of these was Laragh Castle. Four days later he turned up there, much to Iseult Stuart's surprise. After he succeeded in convincing her that he was a friend of her husband's, she agreed to let him stay for a short time and at his request traveled to Dublin and purchased civilian clothing for him at Switzer's on Grafton Street. The Irish Secret Service traced her through store records, and late in May she was arrested. Iseult remained in prison on remand until her trial before the Special Criminal Court on July 1, 1940, at which time the tribunal cleared her of any direct involvement in intelligence activities and ordered her release. Even though the charges against her were dismissed, the trial almost certainly had the effect for many of removing any residual doubts about Stuart's Nazi sympathies.

Stuart produced one book that first year in Germany, a short study of Roger Casement based on William

Maloney's *The Forged Casement Diaries* (1936). Maloney presents the thesis that the diaries, which revealed in graphic detail that the patriot-martyr of 1916 was a homosexual, were fabricated by the English in order to smooth the way for Casement's execution. The Germans were understandably interested in having Maloney's book translated, but when the author demurred, Stuart accepted an invitation to prepare a manuscript advancing the same idea, which could then be translated into German. The result was the book *Der Fall Casement: Das Leben Sir Roger Casements und der Verleumdungsfeldzug des Secret Service.*

While the work does not necessarily reflect Stuart's views in all cases, it does offer some insight into his relationship with the Irish nationalist movement. On the last page, where Stuart is clearly speaking for himself, he wrote:

> Casement's name is now immortal in the history of Ireland—raised high over the reach of the repugnant slander of English forgers. . . .
> Perhaps one day, no longer lying far away, Irish and German soldiers will stand together before [Casement's] unmarked grave . . . to honor the great patriot who has done so much to further friendship between the two nations.

In its anti-British sentiment and its emphasis on the natural alignment of Ireland and Germany, the passage seems the epitome of I.R.A. thinking, at least the thinking of a sizable segment of that organization. Stuart clearly shared at least this view with the nationalist army—whether he shared others is difficult to determine. (Stephen Hayes, the Chief of Staff of the

I.R.A., had commissioned Stuart to carry a message to German authorities requesting that a liaison officer and a radio transmitter be sent to Ireland; and presumably Captain Goertz was dispatched in response to this request. But there is no evidence that Stuart carried out any further activities on the direct behalf of the I.R.A. during the war.)

Stuart's only imaginative work to appear during the war years was the play *Strange Guest,* which was performed at the Abbey in December 1940. His first play, *Men Crowd Me Round,* had a chilly reception at the same theater in 1933. Joseph Holloway, the eccentric Dublin theater dilettante, noted in his diary that only a few had called for the playwright after the performance, "Yeats, Robinson, and a few others." Stuart, it would seem, had shocked the puritan sensibilities of his audience. With great indignation Holloway cited the phrase, "A bloody English bitch," as the quintessence of the author's vulgarity, adding, "I record the vile words to show how far Stuart dared to go." Stuart was understandably bitter over the reception: "I watched from the gallery a few figures scattered through the stalls, sitting upright and rigid. 'A play that should not have been allowed to be produced in a Catholic city,' one critic wrote. The truth was that it was not a play for a city of the dead." *Strange Guest* fared better. Exploring the impact of a sincerely devout individual on an upper middleclass family (one not unlike that of the author's cousins in Antrim), Stuart points up the spiritual emptiness of the Charters family and suggests the means by which new life can be breathed into it. In a way, *Strange Guest* is as explosive a play as *Men Crowd Me Round.* Its failure to shock was perhaps an indication that the audience simply failed to see itself reflected in the Charters. Even Holloway approved of it.

In 1941 Stuart accepted a part-time position as a translator of German news items for broadcast to England. He took the job to ensure that he would be able to continue sending money back to his wife in the event he decided to go to Russia—a possibility he had begun to take seriously, since he had come more and more to see Stalin as possessing the dark Dostoevskian stature Hitler lacked. But the German invasion of Russia in late June effectively put an end to such thoughts. He nonetheless continued the translations for nearly a year, ending them early in 1942.

On a typical day he would meet his classes at Berlin University, and afterward, in the early evening, cross Unter den Linden and walk up Charlottenstrasse to the Wireless Service building, where he had a small office. After an hour or two of turning German prose into something resembling B.B.C. English, he would return to his flat by U-Bahn.

At first he had as his secretary at the Wireless Service a young woman whom he had met in the spring of 1940 and with whom he had since been sharing his apartment. When the relationship cooled, Stuart found a new secretary, Gertrud Meissner, a student in the university. Born November 23, 1915, in Danzig, of Kashubian-Catholic parents, Miss Meissner entered Berlin University in January 1940 and met Stuart a short time later. After she came to work in his office late in 1941, a love affair developed that was different from Stuart's earlier ones. It endured.

When Stuart gave up his job at the Wireless

Service, it must have been with a sense of relief at having finished with broadcast activities. As it turned out, though, he was not finished at all. The most significant effect of having written the talks for William Joyce and prepared the translations was that it now proved awkward to refuse to write and deliver his own talks to Ireland. That Stuart was not eager to be drawn into still another, and even more damning, kind of entanglement is revealed in the July 16, 1942, entry in his Berlin diary: "Talking with [Dr. Hans] Hartmann on telephone and asked to give a twice weekly broadcast from the Irische Redaktion. Said I would let him know in a day or two. It is difficult (though not impossible) to refuse." Stuart eventually agreed, feeling that the action was justified to help offset the flood of English propaganda pouring into Ireland and to encourage Ireland's continued neutrality. It was, of course, a momentous decision, a last decisive step into the dim alleyway of collaboration.

The talks, which were introduced by Miss Meissner and given once a week for well over a year, were by no means the usual fare offered by broad asters on both sides. Cant and moral recrimination were notably absent. On August 1, 1942, Stuart wrote that "these talks must not try to argue, or be clever, or attack too much, or score off other speakers. . . . It is a question of warmth of heart, that first and then the ideas, the 'vision' . . . that springs from this warmth of emotion." Many of the three-to-five minute broadcasts were literary or semiliterary. He read poems by Padraic Pearse, as well as some of his own, and on one St. Patrick's day presented a play he had written on the blind Gaelic poet Raftery. Other talks were largely commentaries on transient news items, though probably often reflecting the German point of view. And still others dealt specifically with Irish affairs. One or two of these had been suggested by Stuart's friend Frank Ryan, an I.R.A. leader who, by a strange twist of fate, was stranded in Germany after fighting against Franco during the Spanish Civil War. Stuart touched on such issues as the execution of I.R.A. members in Northern Ireland and similar executions and imprisonments in the south. During the 1943 general election in Ireland, he advised against supporting Eamon de Valera because of the Irish leader's attitude toward I.R.A. prisoners. This in turn resulted in an official protest to the German Foreign Office by the Irish Chargé d'Affaires in Berlin, William Warnock, on June 1, 1943.

Stuart delivered his talks from Berlin until the spring of 1943 when, because of the increased severity of Allied bombing, broadcast operations were moved to Luxembourg. It was in Luxembourg, while on leave from Berlin University, that he began to experience difficulties with his superiors. Up to this time he had been given virtually complete freedom in the choice of topics and his approach to them. Now, with Germany's growing desperation, there was official pressure to deal with certain subjects, most notably the menace of Russia. At first Stuart ignored the requests, and then, when that became impossible, he stopped broadcasting altogether early in 1944. That spring he and Miss Meissner made their way back to Berlin, large portions of which now lay in ruins.

In September Stuart and the young woman left Berlin in the hope of eventually finding their way out of Ger-

many. They went first to Munich and stayed there
until February, when Stuart decided to move closer
to the Swiss border in hope of crossing into the neutral
country. They traveled by train and foot to Lindau
on Lake Constance. But without a permanent address
in the region, they were forced to move from town to
town, along with the masses of other hungry and
disheveled refugees, returning to Lindau only every
few days. It was some time later, after Miss Meissner
had found lodgings in Dornbirn, just south of Lake
Constance and across the unmarked Austrian fron-
tier, that there was a semblance of stability. She and
Stuart were there when Germany surrendered in May
1945.

Stuart's efforts to enter Switzerland during the latter stages of the war had proved unsuccessful. After
Germany's fall, he made one attempt to arrange passage
to Ireland for Miss Meissner and himself. In August
1945, leaving her in Dornbirn, he joined a group of
French refugees and succeeded in reaching Paris. After
long periods of waiting, he learned from the Irish Em-
bassy that there was no hope whatever of taking the
young woman to Ireland. During these months in Paris,
he was under considerable pressure from home to return
to Ireland at the earliest opportunity. In answer to
a request for money, Iseult wrote to him at the Hôtel
Copernic on October 17, 1945, and said that several
people were willing to help financially. Then she added:
"But you see, Darling, why I keep reiterating in all my
letters that if and when it is possible for you to come
home you should do so at once. So long as you must stay
abroad they are glad and willing to help, but it would

really be an untenable position for you and me if it became possible for you to get home and you refused." Stuart resisted the pressure, unwilling to consider returning unless Miss Meissner could accompany him.

In early November, after a number of false starts, he made his way back to Dornbirn against the flow of refugees headed into France. Within days of his return, he and Miss Meissner were arrested by French occupation troops, cursorily interrogated, and moved to a prison in nearby Bregenz on November 22, 1945. The following May, they were transferred to Freiburg and held by the French in an occupied villa until their unexpected release in July 1946.

The precise reasons for the arrest remain cloudy, since no formal charges were ever brought against Stuart. The most likely explanation is that the French were acting on instructions from London and that the arrest resulted from Stuart's broadcasts to Ireland. Under international law, however, such broadcasts made by a citizen of a neutral country and directed to that neutral country are entirely proper. In other words, Stuart was, it would seem, detained illegally.

The end of imprisonment did not greatly improve their situation. After their release, Stuart and his companion moved to a flat on Schwarzwaldstrasse in Freiburg and remained there until the summer of 1949, dependent much of the time on food parcels from America. For Stuart the wartime experiences, the eight-month imprisonment, and the years in Freiburg had a profound effect. In several of the early novels he had traced his central characters through the tragic pattern of security, vulnerability, and crucifixion, and he had recognized intuitively the value of suffering in leading one to deeper levels of awareness. Now he had moved through the pattern himself, had become one of the despised, and had experienced the harsh reality of suffering. The influence on his later work was indelible. Many of the postwar novels deal with the experiences directly, and all of the others are deeply colored by them. They are the works of a man who has had his glimpse of hell and who is trying to come to terms with his vision. The result is a new sense of understanding, a new capacity for feeling, and a deeper artistry, which unmistakably set the later works apart from the earlier ones.

The artistic transformation brought about by Stuart's experiences in Germany is clearly evident in the first postwar novel, *The Pillar of Cloud*, written in his crowded Freiburg flat and published in England by Victor Gollancz in 1948. Unlike so many of his previous books, this one is the product of an imagination tempered by solid experience and strong emotional involvement. It is something, one suspects, that had to be written, not out of any dream of altering the world but out of an overwhelming need to find some design amid the chaos.

The compulsive nature of the writing and the immediacy of the experiences led Stuart to his mature style. While there are distinct traces of the poetic prose of D. H. Lawrence and the moral tension of Dostoevsky's novels, Stuart is writing for himself; the influences have been well assimilated. One need not read far in *The Pillar of Cloud* to be aware of the stylistic change. The book opens with this passage: "Snow had fallen in the night and covered the ruins. It was bitterly cold as the tall, thin man, who, by his loose and lanky movements, by the very way his worn winter coat hung on him, could be seen to be a foreigner, entered a large undamaged building at the corner of the street." Stuart is creating a poetic atmosphere here, indeed a symbolic atmosphere. Details are chosen not so much for their factualness as for their overtones.

Next to style, perhaps the most striking advance made in the novel lies in the author's attitude toward religion. As we have seen, Stuart noted in his Berlin diary that there had always been an obsession with religion in his books but that it had been "too mental." In short, he had failed to commit himself emotionally. The war changed this: "What has happened to me," he wrote in 1942, "is like a second conversion. The first conversion was at Ballycoyle in 1926 [where he read Underhill's *Mysticism*] but it was an illumination of the mind." Set in the fictional German town of Marheim, *The Pillar of Cloud* describes the gradual development of Dominic Malone's capacity for love, sacrifice, and compassion. Dominic, an Irish poet, has lived through the unsettling days of the war and has been partially changed. He recognizes that his earlier life in Ireland had been complacent and egocentric. Yet much remains unclear to him and true insight evolves slowly. The first faint perception comes after he meets Halka Mayersky. Like Sonya in *Crime and Punishment*, Halka had been forced into prostitution out of necessity, and, like her, she retains her innocence. During the war she had been in a concentration camp and later in an asylum, where she had to endure the horror of electroshock treatments. It is through her experiences that Dominic is led down into the terrible reality of pain and suffering. Nonetheless, it is not until he is himself arrested by the French as a political suspect that real insight develops. The violation of the search, the probing interrogations, and the endless hours of waiting in a grimy cell lead to a new understanding. He comes to see that life can be good if one grasps "the secret of real communion—not just physical contact or even friendship, but fraternity; and especially fraternity with a woman." Upon his release he sets about establishing such a spiritual relationship with Halka and her younger sister, Lisette. Dominic's inner development is not complete, however, until he is able to feel real compassion for Lisette, who is suffering from acute tuberculosis. Although he loves Halka, he finally brings himself to marry Lisette in the hope that he can take her to Ireland, where she might have a chance to recover. The plan proves futile when she dies before permission to leave the country is granted, but his action, involving sacrifice and self-lessness, is a sign of his spiritual maturity.

While *The Pillar of Cloud* is a deeply personal book, tracing Stuart's own spiritual odyssey, it is also a religious parable of unusual power, pointing the way to the only hope left in a world in which the inmate of the asylum becomes the true measure of sanity. The hope he expresses is by no means the superficial kind that ignores the incredible horror of existence; it is a hope born of confrontation with the seemingly endless chaos. What makes Dominic, and Stuart, so different from others who have witnessed the tragic events of this century is the unshakable conviction that goodness can still endure, that one can actually live by Christ's admonition to "Love one another as I have loved you." In this book, which seemed to flow from his pen, unforced and limpid, Stuart has created a song—like the poem Dominic writes in it—at once old and new and, one must add, beautiful and terrifying.

His next novel, *Redemption,* also written in Freiburg and published in 1949, is at least as powerful. Some critics have called it, with justification, Stuart's finest novel, but such an estimate depends on whether one prefers a more consciously artistic and less overtly philosophical work to a book like *The Pillar of Cloud.* Perhaps it is enough to say that both novels are very good.

Unlike *The Pillar of Cloud,* which was conceived and written after the war, *Redemption* has roots that go back to the summer of 1942, when Stuart first tried to begin the novel. He saw the story then as centering on a parish priest and considered having "a state of distaste for everything" as "the prelude to . . . illumination." Stuart was unable, however, to make headway with the book; he noted at one point in his diary that he was starting for the tenth time and the novel remained little more than an idea for the next five years. But the crucial experiences of these years and the firm artistic footing he had discovered with *The Pillar of Cloud* gave him the confidence to make a fresh start on it in Freiburg. The novel is about an Irishman, Ezra Arrigho, who has gone back to his native country after experiencing the fear and agony of wartime Germany; and the plot focuses on Ezra's hesitant progression from

bitterness and despair to something as close to illumination as modern man is likely to find. Estranged from
his Irish wife, Nancy, and bitter over the presumed
death of the girl he loved in Germany, Ezra has brought
with him to Ireland a vivid awareness of destruction and
cruelty. An odor of death clings to him and isolates him
from nearly everyone else in the secure, passionless, and
respectable community of Altamont. There are only two
people with whom he finds it possible to talk: one is the
parish priest, Father Mellowes, who feels that Ezra has
something important to reveal, and the other is Kavanagh, a Dublin fish dealer with branch shops in Altamont, whose distaste for the conventional life is equal-
led only by Ezra's. Both are passionate men, though in
very different ways. The priest is a man of quiet but
intense spirituality, and Kavanagh a man of baser passions, which reveal themselves in his coarse lust.

It is Kavanagh in particular who is moved by the violent and erotic account of Ezra's life during the war.
He senses that there is a whole world outside where
all is permitted, and he becomes convinced of the necessity to stir the waters in what he calls this "duck pond"
of a town. His first taste of Altamont's conventional
morality had come when the local authorities forced
his mistress, Annie Lee, to leave her job at the fish shop.
The intense anger this generates, together with the
vision Ezra has revealed, incites him to strike back at
the community. He instructs Annie, now employed
by Father Mellowes, to place drops of her blood on
the priest's lithograph of St. Francis—thus to "dese-
crate their little pieties with her body and blood," and
to "slake his lust by befouling their miserable altars!"

Although pious townspeople, except Father Mellowes, mistake the desecration for a genuine miracle, Kavanagh is not satisfied; his anger burns just as strongly. He tries to spend his fury by making brutal love to Annie near a desolate railway siding, where "the heavy, dark trucks loomed over them on their iron wheels, in a kind of motionless brutality of couplings and axles." This too fails to satisfy. Nearly a week later he takes Annie back to the siding, as she tortures him with stories of all the men who have possessed her, including the boy who works in Kavanagh's shop, by whom she is pregnant. Kavanagh's anger and lust at last find release here, amid the excrement and mud, when, poised over her, he seizes the knife he had mistakenly left in his pocket and slides it into her body like a rigid, metallic phallus.

This scene, reminiscent of the one describing the axe murders in *Crime and Punishment*, marks a crucial turn in the plot. As in Dostoevsky, it is the consequences of the act, rather than the crime itself, that are of principal importance. Kavanagh had succeeded, almost by accident, in stirring up the duck pond, and the wash of the water reaches everyone. For the ordinary person the crime is little more than something sensational to talk about, like the "miracle" of the picture. For others, like Father Mellowes, and even more so for his sister, Romilly, it is a first stage of initiation into that terrifying reality Ezra had witnessed and described.

Most revealing is the effect it has on Ezra. He had frequently and loudly voiced his contempt for the safe life of those around him, but subconsciously he had been drawn to it and had been in fact living it for about a year. When Kavanagh comes to him with news of the murder, all is suddenly and jarringly changed; for whatever illusions of inviolate security he had nurtured are now utterly shattered. Left psychologically exposed, he withdraws behind a wall of indifference which, ironically, makes it possible for him to commit an act that has an eerie similarity to Kavanagh's. When the priest's sister comes willingly to his room and allows him to make love to her, he is shockingly brutal, intent only on destroying her virginity and respectability. Significantly, during intercourse- Romilly thinks of "Annie in the dark and mud, and the knife going into her."

Ezra had come to the small town to escape the grotesque shadows of evil only to find he has failed to do so, for the calm, sunlit streets of Altamont have their shadows too. Evil is not, as Ezra believes, something outside, like an encircling forest; it exists potentially in every human heart and consequently cannot be escaped. Only Father Mellowes seems at least dimly aware of this; in fact, he says to Ezra after Kavanagh's crime: "And now that you find that the forest, as you called it, is here after all, you don't like it and you want to fly from it, but you can't fly from what's in yourself."

Kavanagh and Ezra have become participants in evil, and Romilly and Father Mellowes have found their lives changed by it. For all of them, there is a sense of pervading chaos. Even the priest—the one person with some understanding of the darkness, is deeply shaken by what has happened and moved to the verge of doubt and despair. After talking with Ezra about Romilly's night with him, Father Mellowes enters a bathroom in Flood's Hotel, where both Kavanagh and Ezra are staying. The room has not been cleaned since the revelries following the previous night's dog races, and it is here, amid lipstick-stained towels, cigarette ends dissolving in the bath, and the stench of vomit, that his anguish reaches its peak: "This is the end, thought the priest, the night of the dog. The words of life turning into a canine howl in the night."

Yet, as so often in Stuart's novels, suffering and the awareness of evil are not an end but a necessary prelude to clear spiritual insight. While Ezra is primarily responsible for leading the characters down into the abyss, it is Father Mellowes, with his simple and natural goodness, who is largely responsible for leading them out. The events of the previous week or so have made him momentarily doubt the power of goodness, but they have not made him withdraw into himself and become unfeeling. He decides to go to live above Kavanagh's fish shop with his sister and Kavanagh, who has not as yet been arrested; and he invites Ezra to join them, telling him: "Isn't it time . . . that we forgave each other? Perhaps this is our last chance to lead a new life and if we don't take it there won't be another." Father Mellowes's capacity for love, compassion, and forgiveness is indication enough that the words of life have not totally degenerated "into a canine howl in the night."

Ezra is at first reluctant to accept the priest's idea. He does not believe that the members of the proposed group have much in common, nor does he have much faith in "love one another." But there have been signs that he is at last ready for such fraternity. Margareta, the girl whom he had thought killed during a bombing raid in Germany, manages to locate him after spending a long period in a refugee camp. She had been injured during the raid and left a cripple, who, she says, is "not nice to sleep with now." Ezra's willingness to accept her as she is indicates his own capacity for love and compassion. Moreover, he is now able to see his own likeness in Kavanagh and to sense that there is "no final wall between his blood and Kavanagh's blood, his flesh and Kavanagh's flesh." From this perception, it is not far to the eventual realization that what the members of the priest's group will share is a common humanity and common experience of the darkness. Hence Ezra agrees to live in the flat above the shop, even while questioning its value.

Stuart has long maintained that what hope there is lies in just such gatherings, in which the members are bound by love, understanding, and shared suffering—fraternity. This was the idea lying behind the proposed colonies in *Pigeon Irish,* and it is the idea behind the almost familial relationship that evolves in *The Pillar of Cloud* and *Redemption.* While it is possible (perhaps even right) to say that this concept emerged from Stuart's longing for the kind of close family relationship he was denied as a child, one must observe that the solution is universal and not merely personal.

The strength of the kind of small community Stuart has in mind is that, by submitting to the group, one is in effect subordinating the flesh to the spirit. The matter is presented symbolically in *Redemption* when Romilly marries Kavanagh just before his arrest in order to be able to visit and comfort him during his imprisonment.

It is in fact a marriage of spirit and flesh. The unity that results has its counterpart in a vision of reality that brings together a knowledge of evil and a knowledge of goodness.

Redemption does not conclude with a sudden flash of metaphysical insight and certainty. After Kavanagh's execution, Ezra is still unsure enough of the existence of divine purpose to ask Father Mellowes: "All the destructive pain, what can come of it? . . . Can there be any point in it or isn't it the sign of chaos?" The answer comes not in words but in the gentle smile of the priest; Ezra senses that this is as close to a final revelation as any of them will ever come—but it is enough. For like Guard Higgins, the Altamont policeman who has discovered a strain of grass that will thrive in the hostile environment of mountains and bogs, Ezra, Father Mellowes, and the others have discovered in the group something capable of flourishing in the wastes of the modern world.

By the time *Redemption* was published, Stuart had given up any idea of returning to Ireland, partly because he had been led to believe that Sean MacBride, Iseult's half-brother and the Irish Minister of External Affairs, would not look favorably on a new application. Finally, in the summer of 1949, Stuart returned to France and succeeded, with the help of friends, in arranging for Miss Meissner to come to Paris as a maid. After she arrived, they lived in an attic supplied by the writer Ladislas Dormandi.

During the nearly two years they spent in Paris, from 1949 to the spring of 1951, Stuart completed one novel, *The Flowering Cross,* which appeared in July 1950.

Thematically, the book is cut from the same cloth as the two previous works. Once more the question of salvation lies at the center, and Stuart again suggests that man finds salvation only after intense struggle and suffering and only after opening his heart to others.

The plot in this case forms around the sculptor Louis Clancy, who has experienced ignominy and suffering during imprisonment in France and who has furthermore experienced the tenderness of Alyse, a blind girl imprisoned with him. He senses that Alyse, innocent and comforting, offers an alternative to the dreadful sense of chaos he feels. She becomes for him the flowering cross.

While the book lacks the intensity of the earlier postwar novels, it nonetheless offers a particularly revealing insight into Stuart's attitude toward his own work and toward the artist in general. Louis, like Stuart, is one of those who have passed through the depths, and he works "at forming clay figures that [have] a tangible little core of resistance to the chaotic passions and lusts and miseries." The end of art for him is not financial success or even recognition, but the creation of a form containing this core of resistance to the surrounding chaos:

> What we can put against the petty sensuality of the streets isn't idealism or spirituality, it's the tangible body of Christ as He stood there in the dusk by His beloved lake, come to turn a few evenings sweet with the touch of His hands, kindling a fire or grilling a fish. That is the stilled, tender, death-embracing sensuality, and I try to make a shadow of it fall over my little figures.

There is perhaps no clearer expression of Stuart's art, especially his postwar art, than is found here.

During most of the first three years of their stay in London, to which Stuart and Miss Meissner had gained entry in the spring of 1951, they lived at 4 Sinclair Gardens in a drab part of Kensington. Financially at least, the years here were among the very worst Stuart had ever experienced. Miss Meissner as an alien was permitted to do only poorly paid domestic work, and just to meet the weekly rent Stuart was forced to take a variety of uninspiring jobs, which included sorting Christmas mail in an auxiliary post office, and working in an all-night cable office in Picadilly and as a warder at the Geological Museum in South Kensington. Even with the jobs, however, their financial position was tenuous and at times desperate.

The uncongenial atmosphere of middleclass Kensington, the nagging worries about money, and the distractions of the many jobs hardly proved conducive to any major artistic achievement. It was perhaps inevitable that the two books Stuart wrote during the period turned out to be among his weakest. *Good Friday's Daughter,* published in 1952, is set in Ireland and contrasts the lives of two brothers: Mark, who succumbs to the flesh by carrying on an affair with his brother's wife, Danielle, and who finds only emptiness and destruction; and Leo, who ultimately achieves fulfillment in a tiny community composed of his sick mother and Antonia, the girl he loves. In *The Chariot,* published the next year, the scene shifts to London, and once again the principal concern is with the formation of a small group, which consists this time of Amos, a neglected novelist; Lena, a former prostitute; and Lena's invalid mother. The shortcomings of both books are painfully evident. In *Good Friday's Daughter,* for instance, one winces at the melodramatic suicides of Mark and Danielle, who leap from a cliff and are later discovered, quite improbably, in a grotesque embrace. And in *The Chariot*, it is hard not to question the appropriateness of linking a wheel-chair with William Blake's "chariot of fire." Such flaws as these, together with the generally uninspired prose, are all the more difficult to accept coming so soon after the sure artistry of *The Pillar of Cloud* and *Redemption*.

Between 1954 and 1958 life in London eased some-what for Stuart. On March 22, 1954, Iseult Stuart died of a coronary thrombosis after a lingering illness, and her death made it possible for him to marry Miss Meissner. The marriage, which took place in May, improved their financial situation considerably, since, as his wife, Gertrud was permitted to take better paying clerical work in a fabric firm and later in the foreign department of a bank. Moreover, they moved to a less expensive flat above a store at 63 Barking Road near the docks in London's East End. Though rough and noisy, the neighborhood had a vitality that Stuart much preferred to the deadness of Kensington. The lower rent here and the improved income from his wife's jobs removed much of Stuart's anxiety over money and freed him to devote more time to his writing.

The novels that came out of these later years in London, *The Pilgrimage* (1955) and *Victors and Vanquished* (1958), show some improvement over the preceding two, but they nonetheless fall far short of his best work. While the themes remain basically the same, there does not seem to be the vital energy that lay behind a book like *Redemption*. Stuart himself gives perhaps the best explanation for the decline in power, a decline that is remarkably like that evident in the later prewar novels: "I am one of those writers who identify themselves closely with their fiction. This has a bearing on the fact that it has been at the start of a creative phase that I have written at my best; it has been out of a pressure of stored living and experiencing." One might add that as the experience and the writing grew farther apart, emotion began to dominate and distort his work. So it is that Stuart's fascination with disease, clear enough in such books as *The Pillar of Cloud, Redemption,* and *The Flowering Cross,* verges on morbid obsession in *The Pilgrimage,* culminating in the rape of the seriously ill Chaton by two brothers, one of whom is crippled. Similarly in *Victors and Vanquished,* the tenderness that was handled well in the first three postwar books comes dangerously close to sentimentality in the relationship between Luke Cassidy and the abandoned child he cares for.

In April 1958, the same month *Victors and Vanquished* appeared in print, Stuart brought his life full circle by returning to Ireland to live. The decision to come back was by no means sudden. His marriage had eliminated the difficulties of bringing Gertrud into the country, yet they had stayed on in London for another four years. Understandably, after all that had happened to him over the past twenty years, there were some doubts about returning. Stuart commented in a 1970 interview that during the early days in Germany he had at times been homesick but that in the later war years he had had "a feeling of not wishing to come back [to Ireland] at all." This feeling, though, gradually gave way.

From the time they returned in 1958 to 1971 Stuart

lived in a small cottage, The Reask, located near the village of Dunshaughlin in County Meath. Here, with his wife and his mother, who lived with them until her death in 1960, he again succeeded in establishing his own kind of intimate community. What this new life meant to him is imaginatively embodied in the *Angels of Providence,* published in 1959: the pleasure of making their home a part of themselves, the simple delight in unearthing ancient paving stones near their well, and the sense of warmth and fulfillment in the small group. Like Amos in *The Chariot* Stuart had managed to re-create "the world before the wonder went out of it."

The twelve years Stuart spent in the comparative seclusion of County Meath were scarcely among his most productive. After *Angels of Providence,* not another book appeared during the period. The silence was broken only by a play, *Flynn's Last Dive,* which was performed in the London suburb of Croydon at the experimental Pembroke Theatre in March 1962. Yet this work, one of his better dramatic efforts, was hardly proof that he had regained his creative energies. He produced nothing else until eight years later.

In 1970, at the age of sixty-eight, Stuart accepted a commission from the directors of the Abbey Theatre to write a play commemorating the fiftieth anniversary of Irish Republican Terence MacSwiney's death while on a hunger strike in Brixton jail, London. Someone who did not know Stuart well might have thought he would take this modest form of official recognition, coming so late in his career, with proper grace and turn out the usual kind of emasculated commemorative piece, which was apparently what was called for. Stuart, however, was never one to do the expected, and this occasion proved no exception. Instead of writing the ordinary banalities about a safely dead national hero, he took MacSwiney's life and words and used them as an ideal against which to measure, with satirical pointedness, the materialism and spiritual vacuity of modern Ireland. It is very likely that MacSwiney himself, could he have been called upon, would have applauded the intention, but the Abbey directors found little to applaud and canceled the play, *Who Fears to Speak,* during rehearsals because it was "unsuitable." The directors did not elaborate on their summary decision, but it is clear in a letter to the playwright from Thomas MacAnna, the play's producer and staunch defender, that the rejection was due to the political implications of the work. Shortly after the cancellation, Stuart commented to *The Irish Press:* "Were this a purely personal matter as between me and the Abbey directors, I should accept it as one of the hazards of the life of an outspoken writer. But as one who believes that MacSwiney should be sincerely and properly honoured at this time, and not just accorded the usual ritualistic lip-service, I shall do all I can to this end." He was true to his word. The play, whose title now took on a peculiar irony, was given a stage reading at Liberty Hall on December 1, 1970. As was usually the case with Stuart's works, the notices were decidedly mixed, ranging from a pillorying by *The Irish Times,* which called it "strangled in narrative and rhetoric, deadened by political propagandising and utterly devoid of any recognised form of human life," to the accolades of

The Irish Press, which saw it as "a brilliant theatrical conception," indeed "a coup-de-theatre."

In August 1971, Stuart and his wife left their cottage in Meath and moved to a new home in the Windy Arbour section of Dublin. Four months later he published his twentieth novel, *Black List, Section H*, which Lawrence Durrell has called "a book of the finest imaginative distinction." Without doubt *Black List* is Stuart's best novel since *Redemption* and quite possibly his best ever. Whether it marks the beginning of still another major phase in his work or a very distinguished ending to his long career, only time will tell. But one thing is certain: the novel does not have the air of a *nunc dimittis*.

Stuart has called *Black List* a "memoir in fictional form," and the description is apt. Closely autobiographical, and yet written with something bordering on mystical detachment, the novel traces the author's life from the time he left Rugby through most of his postwar imprisonment. It tells of his relationship with Yeats, Maud Gonne, Iseult, and Gertrud (all but the last of whom appear under their real names); of his feelings toward Ireland during the Civil War and Germany during World War II; it tells of violence and tenderness, happiness and pain. All the major themes of his work are recapitulated: the belief that the artist must be ever vigilant, constantly questioning, a counterforce to the stale assumptions of society; the conviction that through suffering comes true insight, that through opening one's heart to others the spirit and the flesh may become one, that there is a goodness in the world to be set next to the vision of chaos.

Yet *Black List* is more than a powerful and imaginative recounting of the author's life and thought. H, the central character, is quite obviously Stuart (whose unused first name is Henry), but the kind of pilgrimage he undertakes is one of universal significance. His search for meaning in an unstable world is no less than the search every man must make if he wishes to discover more in life than overwhelming despair or, even worse, deathlike monotony.

Should this remarkable novel turn out to be his last, which one hopes is not the case, it will be a fitting capstone to a career that had begun inconspicuously enough with the ragged volume of poetry Yeats had liked, moved through the interesting but tentative experimentation of such novels as *Pigeon Irish* and *The Coloured Dome,* and reached a rich maturity in *The Pillar of Cloud* and *Redemption.* Through all these years Stuart has remained a thoroughly dedicated artist, constantly fascinated by the difficult; his failures resulted not from any betrayal of his art but from an inability to fulfill the complex tasks he set for himself. It seems inevitable that in due time, when the good is finally sifted from the bad, several of Francis Stuart's novels, including *Black List,* will rank very high in the fiction of modern Ireland and that he will find at last his just place as one of Ireland's truly significant writers.

Selected Bibliography

PRIMARY SOURCES

Books

We Have Kept the Faith. Dublin: Oak Leaf Press, 1923. [Title page reads H. Stuart.]

Women and God. London: Jonathan Cape, 1931.

Pigeon Irish. London: Victor Gollancz, 1932. New York: Macmillan, 1932.

The Coloured Dome. London: Victor Gollancz, 1932. New York: Macmillan, 1933.

Try the Sky. Foreword by Compton Mackenzie. London: Victor Gollancz, 1933. New York: Macmillan, 1933.

Glory. London: Victor Gollancz, 1933. New York: Macmillan, 1933.

Things to Live For: Notes for an Autobiography. London: Jonathan Cape, 1934. New York: Macmillan, 1935.

In Search of Love. London: Collins, 1935. New York: Macmillan, 1935.

The Angel of Pity. London: Grayson and Grayson, 1935.

The White Hare. London: Collins, 1936. New York: Macmillan, 1936.

The Bridge. London: Collins, 1937.

Julie. London: Collins, 1938. New York: Knopf, 1938.

The Great Squire. London: Collins, 1939.

Der Fall Casement: Das Leben Sir Roger Casements und der Verleum-

dungsfeldzug des Secret Service. Translated by Ruth Weiland. Hamburg: Hanseatische, [1940].

The Pillar of Cloud. London: Victor Gollancz, 1948.

Redemption. London: Victor Gollancz, 1949. New York: Devin-Adair, 1950.

The Flowering Cross. London: Victor Gollancz, 1950.

Good Friday's Daughter. London: Victor Gollancz, 1952.

The Chariot. London: Victor Gollancz, 1953.

The Pilgrimage. London: Victor Gollancz, 1955.

Victors and Vanquished. London: Victor Gollancz, 1958. Cleveland: Pennington Press, 1959.

Angels of Providence. London: Victor Gollancz, 1959.

Black List, Section H. Preface and Postscript by Harry T. Moore. Carbondale: Southern Illinois University, 1971. London: Feffer and Simons, 1971.

Plays (unpublished)

Men Crowd Me Round. Presented at the Abbey Theatre, March 1933.

Glory. Presented at the Arts Theatre Club, London, January 1936. [Dramatized version of the novel.]

Strange Guest. Presented at the Abbey Theatre, December 1940.

Flynn's Last Dive. Presented at the Pembroke Theatre, Croydon, March 1962.

Who Fears To Speak. Presented at Liberty Hall, Dublin, December 1970.

Manuscripts

Carter, Carolle J. Interview with Francis Stuart, 1969.

Natterstad, J.H. Interview with Francis Stuart, 1970.

Stuart, Francis. Berlin diary, 1942.

———. Letters to F.R. Higgins, 1935. National Library of Ireland (Ms. 10,864).

———. Letters to J.H. Natterstad, 1969–72.

———. Letters to Joseph O'Neill, 1934–1935. National Library of Ireland (Ms. 8184).

————. Notebooks; typescripts of *Victors and Vanquished, Strange Guest,* and *Flynn's Last Dive;* and manuscript of *Black List, Section H.* Morris Library, Southern Illinois University at Carbondale. [The collection at Morris Library also contains letters to Francis Stuart from Liam O'Flaherty, Iseult Stuart, Ethel Mannin, and others.]

SECONDARY SOURCES

Bibliography

Mc Cormack, W.J. "Francis Stuart: A Checklist and Commentary." *Long Room,* no. 3 (Spring 1971), pp. 38–49.

Criticism

d'Astorg, Bertrand. "Le Roman des Ruines, Le Sacre Renaitra." *Esprit,* no. 186 (January 1952), pp. 145–50. [Review essay.] Reprinted in *Aspects de la Littérature Européenne dupuis 1945.* Paris: Éditions du Seuil, 1952.

Goldberg, Helen. *Women and God; a Study of Francis Stuart.* M.A. thesis, New York University, 1956.

Greene, David H. "The Return of Francis Stuart." *Envoy* 5 (August 1951): 10–21.

Kiely, Benedict, *Modern Irish Fiction—A Critique.* Dublin: Golden Eagle Books, 1950.

Maxton, Hugh [W. J. Mc Cormack]. "Francis Stuart: The Long-Distance Winner." *Hibernia* 34 (August 28, 1970): 20.

Mc Cormack, W.J., ed. *A Festschrift for Francis Stuart on His Seventieth Birthday.* Dublin: Dolmen Press, 1972.

Mendes, João. "Francis Stuart, Romancista." *Brotéria* 54 (1952): 477–84. [Review essay.]

O'Brien, H. J. "Francis Stuart's Cathleen Ni Houlahan." *Dublin Magazine* 8 (Summer 1971): 48–54.

Radine, Serge. *Lumières dans la Nuit.* Paris: La Colombe, 1956.

Venaissin, Gabriel. "Francis Stuart ou Je Vivrai le Malheur des Autres." *Critique,* no. 86–87 (July–August 1954), pp. 645–56. [Review essay.]